WILDLIFE WORLDS

NORTH AMERICA

TIM HARRIS

CRABTREE
PUBLISHING COMPANY
WWW.CRABTREEBOOKS.COM

Published in Canada
Crabtree Publishing
616 Welland Avenue
St. Catharines, ON
L2M 5V6

Published in the United States
Crabtree Publishing
PMB 59051
350 Fifth Ave, 59th Floor
New York, NY 10118

Published in 2020 by Crabtree Publishing Company

First published in Great Britain in 2019 by The Watts Publishing Group
Copyright © The Watts Publishing Group 2019

Printed in the U.S.A./122019/CG20191101

With thanks to the Nature Picture Library

Author: Tim Harris

Editorial director: Kathy Middleton

Editors: Amy Pimperton, Robin Johnson

Series Designer: Nic Davies smartdesignstudio.co.uk

Photo researchers: Rachelle Morris (Nature Picture Library), Laura Sutherland (Nature Picture Library), Diana Morris

Proofreader: Wendy Scavuzzo

Production coordinator and prepress: Tammy McGarr

Print coordinator: Katherine Berti

Photo credits:
Alamy: David E.Lester 9tl.
Dreamstime: Atomazul 10bl; Anthony Heflin 22c, 31; Irina Kozhemyakina 13bl; Brian Lasenby 19tr; Michal Pešata 21bl; Andrei Gabriel Stanescu 18.
Nature PL: Ingo Arndt 2b, 10–11c,11bl, 20–21c, 21tr; John Cancalosi 7t, 23tr. Philippe Clement 13tr, 18bl; Claudio Contrera 19tl; Michael Durham 25tr; David Fleetham 15tl; Dr Axel Gebauer back cover tr,7bl; Danny Green front cover t; Gavin Hellier 26–27c; Daniel Heuclin 17c; Ole Jorgen Liodden 29c; Barry Mansell 19bl; Larry Michael 23c; Flip Nicklin 28bl; Todd Pusser 27tl; Jouan Rius 6b, 12, 17tl; Charlie Summers 27br; Tom Vezo back cover tl, 9cl, 13tl; Gerrit Vyn 8–9p; Doc White 28c.
Shutterstock: Ad-hominem 5c; James Anderson 27bl, 32b; Bildagenteur Zoonar GmbH 5b; Bill45 6t, 16; Bobs Creek Photography 25t, 32t; miroslav chytil back cover tcr, 4b; Dydo Diem 10t; Rudi Ernst 3b, 13br; FotoRequest 11br, 29tl; C_Gara 29bl; Karin de Jonge-Fotografie 29tr; Chris Kolaczan 26bl; Alex Krassel 15tr; Brian Lasenby 21br; Viktor Loki 7br; magnusdeepbelow 15br; Maria Martyshova front cover c, 1c; Joe McDonald 9cr; MNStudio 3t, 14–15c; Steve Oehlenschlager 21cr; David Osborn 1t, 25br; Bill Perry 3bg, 4–5c, 6t, 32c; PhotoXite 2t, 24–25c; Tom Reichner 3c, 17br, 20l; Nancy S 19br, 30t; Sezai Sahmay back cover tcl, 14bl; Steven Russell Smit front cover b; Jenn Strong 5t; Paul Tessier 23tl; Vara I 24bl; Sista Vongjuntanaruk 8bl; Joe West 15bl, 30b.

Library and Archives Canada Cataloguing in Publication

Title: North America / Tim Harris.
Names: Harris, Tim (Ornithologist), author.
Description: Series statement: Wildlife worlds | Previously published: London: Franklin Watts, 2019. | Includes index.
Identifiers: Canadiana (print) 20190200677 | Canadiana (ebook) 20190200685 | ISBN 9780778776819 (hardcover) | ISBN 9780778776871 (softcover) | ISBN 9781427125354 (HTML)
Subjects: LCSH: Animals—North America—Juvenile literature. | LCSH: Habitat (Ecology)—North America—Juvenile literature. | LCSH: Natural history—North America—Juvenile literature. | LCSH: North America—Juvenile literature.
Classification: LCC QL151 .H37 2020 | DDC j591.97—dc23

Library of Congress Cataloging-in-Publication Data

Names: Harris, Tim (Ornithologist), author.
Title: North America / Tim Harris.
Description: New York : Crabtree Publishing Company, 2020. | Series: Wildlife worlds | Includes index.
Identifiers: LCCN 2019043668 (print) | LCCN 2019043669 (ebook) | ISBN 9780778776819 (hardcover) | ISBN 9780778776871 (paperback) | ISBN 9781427125354 (ebook)
Subjects: LCSH: Animals--North America--Juvenile literature. | Plants--North America--Juvenile literature.
Classification: LCC QL151 .H29 2020 (print) | LCC QL151 (ebook) | DDC 591.97--dc23
LC record available at https://lccn.loc.gov/2019043668
LC ebook record available at https://lccn.loc.gov/2019043669

Contents

North American Continent

North America is Earth's third-largest continent, after Asia and Africa. It is surrounded by oceans, except for a narrow strip of land called the Isthmus of Panama that connects it to South America.

In the far north, Greenland is **permanently** covered by a thick layer of ice, and there are many **glaciers** in the Rocky Mountains. In contrast, some parts of Central America have tropical **rain forests**, and major **deserts** stretch across northern Mexico and the southwestern United States. **Coniferous** forest covers much of Canada, while the gentle Appalachian Mountains have **broad-leaved** woodland.

In such a continent of contrasts, it is not surprising that North America is known for amazing wildlife displays. These include grizzly bears hunting salmon as the fish swim up rivers in Alaska, millions of bats emerging at dusk from caves in Texas, and thousands of birds called herons feeding with sunbathing alligators in the Florida Everglades.

GRIZZLY BEAR

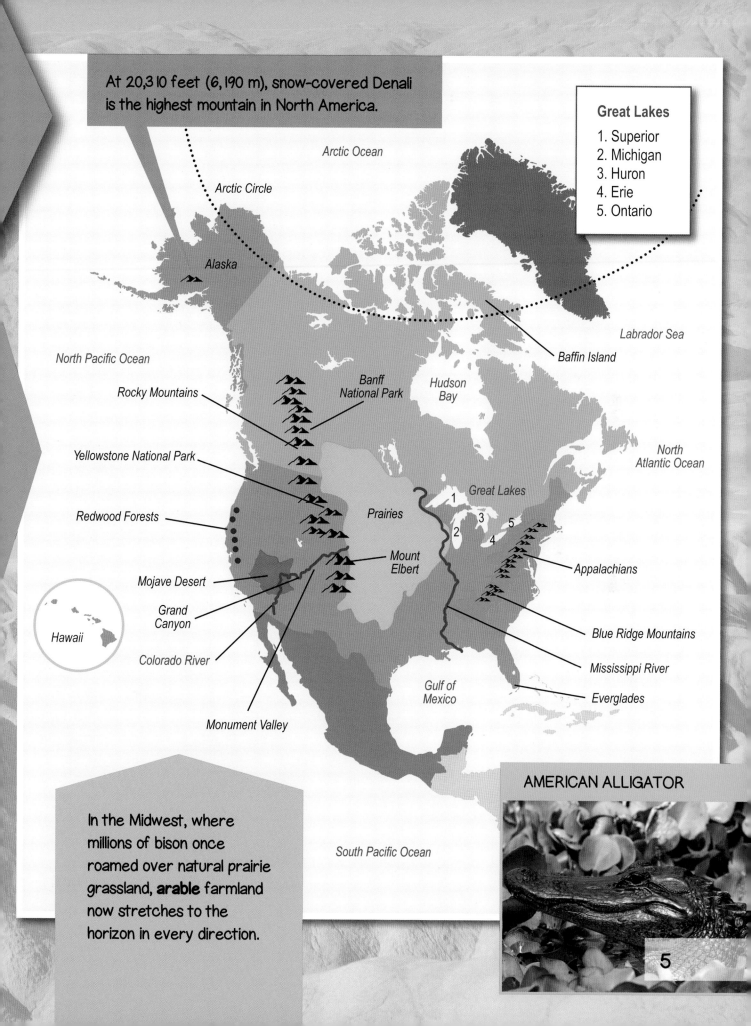

At 20,310 feet (6,190 m), snow-covered Denali is the highest mountain in North America.

Great Lakes

1. Superior
2. Michigan
3. Huron
4. Erie
5. Ontario

Arctic Ocean

Arctic Circle

Alaska

North Pacific Ocean

Labrador Sea

Baffin Island

Hudson Bay

Rocky Mountains

Banff National Park

North Atlantic Ocean

Yellowstone National Park

Redwood Forests

Prairies

Great Lakes

Mount Elbert

Appalachians

Mojave Desert

Grand Canyon

Hawaii

Colorado River

Blue Ridge Mountains

Mississippi River

Everglades

Monument Valley

Gulf of Mexico

In the Midwest, where millions of bison once roamed over natural prairie grassland, **arable** farmland now stretches to the horizon in every direction.

South Pacific Ocean

AMERICAN ALLIGATOR

5

Mojave Desert

The Mojave Desert is a land of rolling sand dunes, rugged mountains, and rocky country covered with creosote bushes and Joshua trees in the southwestern United States. An area of the desert called Death Valley is the lowest, hottest, and driest place in North America.

Animals in the Mojave Desert have adapted to the extreme heat. **Coyotes** are **nocturnal**, emerging from their dens in the cooler evening hours to hunt. Jackrabbits and other small animals shelter under bushes or hide in holes to avoid the Sun's heat. Desert tortoises sleep through the entire summer, waking only when the weather gets cooler in autumn.

DEATH VALLEY

Joshua trees have bare branches with clusters of leaves at the end. Some may live for 1,000 years. Native North Americans make traditional baskets and sandals from the long, thin leaves. The flower buds and seeds can be cooked for food.

Roadrunners rarely fly, but these desert birds can run quicker than the fastest human sprinter. Their favorite meals include spiders, scorpions, and lizards.

Hungry sand scorpions leave their holes at night to find food in the Mojave Desert. They are the largest scorpion species in North America.

The throat of a Costa's hummingbird shines bright purple in sunlight. This little bird feeds on the **nectar** of desert flowers.

Mississippi River

The mighty Mississippi is the third-longest river in the world. It flows more than 2,320 miles (3,733 km) from Lake Itasca in Minnesota south to the Gulf of Mexico. Other large rivers, such as the Missouri, Ohio, and Arkansas, join forces with the Mississippi along its route. Just before it reaches the sea, it splits into many different channels.

People have used the Mississippi River as a transportation route and a source of food for thousands of years. Almost 400 kinds of fish live in its waters, along with freshwater turtles, alligators, wood ducks, and other waterbirds.

Snapping turtles wait for their **prey** in shallow, muddy water.

Water from 31 states drains into the Mississippi as it winds through forests, farmland, and big cities such as Memphis and New Orleans. Close to the sea, the Mississippi River **Delta** contains salt flats, such as those found in Barataria Bay (above).

Green darner dragonflies fly over the Mississippi River, chasing and eating smaller insects.

Wood ducks nest in natural holes in trees so that ducklings (right) stay safe. Male birds (left) have colorful feathers during the breeding season.

Everglades

The Everglades is a wetland in southern Florida so large that it is impossible to see from one side to the other. Despite its size, the water there is so shallow that it only comes up to an average adult's knees.

Millions of fish and other small creatures live in the waters of the Everglades. They attract predators of all kinds. Birds called herons wade through the water, snatching fish with their beaks, while alligators patrol in search of larger prey. Offshore, **manatees** swim in the shallow water, grazing on underwater plants. **Mangrove forests** grow where the fresh water of the Everglades meets the ocean.

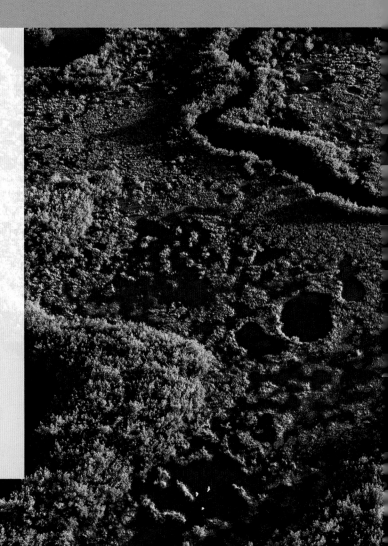

River otters are playful animals covered in thick, velvety fur. They are skilled swimmers who catch fish in the Everglades.

Thousands of herons, including green herons, (right), egrets, and ibis, feed in the shallow waters of the Everglades.

The vast sawgrass **marshes** of the Everglades are sometimes called the "River of Grass."

An American alligator slowly drifts through the shallow water as it looks for a meal.

Grand Canyon

The Grand Canyon is the largest canyon in North America. It cuts through northern Arizona as though a giant knife had sliced through Earth's surface. It is more than 277 miles (446 km) long and up to 18 miles (29 km) wide.

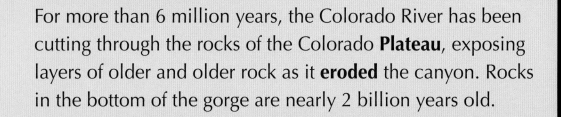

For more than 6 million years, the Colorado River has been cutting through the rocks of the Colorado **Plateau**, exposing layers of older and older rock as it **eroded** the canyon. Rocks in the bottom of the gorge are nearly 2 billion years old.

At is deepest point, the Grand Canyon is more than 6,000 feet (1,829 m) deep. In many places, the canyon walls are **vertical**. This is where the hardest rocks are found. Gentler slopes have formed where there are softer rocks.

Mountain lions, or cougars, hunt for food in the canyon at night.

The bald eagle is the national bird of the United States. These magnificent **birds of prey** hunt trout in the Colorado River.

Clever **camouflage** makes horned lizards difficult to see against rocks in the canyon.

Hawaii

Hawaii is part of a group of islands in the middle of the Pacific Ocean. Very heavy rain falls on the islands between October and April, making Hawaii one of the wettest places on Earth.

Hawaii is built on five volcanoes. Rain forests grow on the lower slopes of the volcanoes. Some of the birds found in these forests live nowhere else in the world. The ocean water around Hawaii is very rich in marine life, including sea turtles, monk seals, dolphins, humpback whales, and many different kinds of fish.

One of Hawaii's volcanoes, Mauna Loa, is the largest volcano on Earth. Another volcano, Kilauea, has erupted almost continuously since 1983, sending **molten lava** streaming down its slopes. The lava cools and hardens. After a few years, plants begin to grow on it.

14

Pom-pom crabs hold marine animals called **sea anemones** in their claws. The anemones gather tiny pieces of food, which the crabs scrape off and eat.

The nene is the world's rarest goose. In the wild, it lives only in Hawaii and on nearby islands.

Although it looks scary, the giant oceanic manta ray is a harmless fish.

The Hawaiian hibiscus grows up to 33 feet (10 m) tall and has bright-yellow flowers.

Monument Valley

On the border between Arizona and Utah, huge stacks of **sandstone** rise high above the desert of Monument Valley. The stacks, called buttes, are colored red by chemicals in the rocks.

In summer, Monument Valley is very hot, but it can be cold enough for snow in winter. At first sight, the valley may look lifeless. But many lizards, jackrabbits, and other creatures live there. They are hunted by predators such as red-tailed hawks, mountain lions, and rattlesnakes.

West Mitten Butte (left) and East Mitten Butte (right) tower above the valley floor. These huge chunks of rock got their names because they look like gigantic mittens.

Leopard lizards have spots like leopards. These small desert reptiles warm their bodies by sunbathing on rocks.

Venomous rattlesnakes scare away predators by shaking the hollow scales at the end of their tails. When shaken, the scales make a rattling noise.

Soapweed yuccas can survive the very dry conditions in Monument Valley. Native North Americans boil and eat the plant's seeds.

17

Redwood Forests

The lush forests that grow near the coast of the Pacific Ocean in northern California have the world's tallest trees. They are called coastal redwoods. The tallest redwood, named Hyperion, was discovered in 2006. It towers about 380 feet (116 m) above the forest floor.

The redwood forests and the rivers that run through them are home to many animals, some of which are rare. They include the northern spotted owl and the Chinook salmon. Other animals that live in the forests include snakes and flying squirrels.

Heavy rains fall during the winter, and fog rolls in from the ocean in summer. Unlike in tropical rain forests, the weather is cool for much of the year but just as wet! The redwoods grow well in that very wet climate.

During the day, Townsend's big-eared bats sleep in caves and old buildings. They wake up at dusk to hunt for flying insects in the forests.

Flying squirrels climb up and down redwood trunks and leap among the branches. They can also glide from tree to tree when they need to.

Ring-necked snakes live on the forest floor. They show their bright underbellies to warn off predators.

During breeding season, male Sierran tree frogs gather by water and call to attract females.

Prairies

An immense "sea" of grass once stretched across most of the North American Midwest. Only a fraction of that natural grassland, called prairies, now remains.

Most of the prairies have been converted to fields for growing wheat or corn, or for cattle ranching. Some shortgrass prairie still grows in the west. In the wetter east, tallgrass prairie grows higher than people, with a carpet of wildflowers beneath. The prairies were once home to millions of bison, but only a few thousand of these huge grazing animals remain.

American bison, or buffalo, spend their days grazing on prairie grasses.

Small purple pasque flowers are the first sign of spring on the prairies, sometimes poking up through snow.

Badlands is a national park found in the praires of South Dakota. Over thousands of years, the soft rocks beneath the park have been worn away by the action of rivers and streams. This erosion has created a dramatic landscape of towering rocks and valleys. There are millions of **fossils** in these rocks, including ancient horses and alligators.

Mixed-grass prairie grows at Badlands. Shortgrass and tallgrass prairies meet there in the middle.

In April, male prairie chickens blow up yellow air sacs on their necks to attract females.

Monarch butterflies come to feed on milkweed when it blooms on the South Dakota prairie.

Blue Ridge Mountains

The Blue Ridge Mountains form part of the Appalachian range. They stretch from Alabama in the south to Pennsylvania in the north. There are 125 peaks that are more than 5,000 feet (1,524 m) high in the mountains. Broad-leaved and coniferous forest covers the **summits**.

Bears, foxes, coyotes, bobcats, deer, and snakes live in the forest. In spring, the songs of thousands of birds echo through the forest. Salamanders and frogs swim in the many streams that flow toward the Great Appalachian Valley on one side and the Atlantic Ocean on the other.

The blue haze that gives the mountains their name hangs over the forest in Shenandoah National Park. A chemical given off by the trees produces the color.

Male wild turkeys have magnificent, fan-shaped tails. They are heavy birds, but they fly well through the forest and often perch high in trees.

The tiny Shenandoah salamander thrives in damp conditions, so it lives only in the higher, wetter parts of the mountains.

Bobcats have tufted ears and stubby tails. They hunt for small animals in the early morning and evening.

Yellowstone National Park

Yellowstone has towering fountains of boiling water, mud pools, colorful hot springs, spectacular waterfalls, and steep-sided canyons. This national park in Wyoming is a vast area of natural wilderness.

Fascinating animals live in the dark pine forests, grasslands, and lakes of Yellowstone. There are lumbering bison, bears, and moose. Herds of wild horses, wolves, mountain lions, and wolverines live there. Eagles, hawks, and many other birds also make their homes in Yellowstone, the oldest national park in North America.

Every hour or so, a **geyser** called Old Faithful shoots boiling water high into the air with a loud whooshing sound. It has erupted more than one million times since it was discovered in 1870.

Herds of wild horses roam across the park's grasslands.

The vivid colors of Grand Prismatic Spring are created by millions of **bacteria** around the edge of the water.

Wolves were reintroduced to Yellowstone in the 1990s. Today, there are about a dozen packs roaming through the park's forests.

Moose are the world's largest deer. The males use their gigantic **antlers** to fight each other.

Rocky Mountains

Hundreds of peaks make up North America's greatest mountain range. The Rocky Mountains stretch more than 3,000 miles (4,830 km) from New Mexico to British Columbia, Canada. The tallest peak is Mount Elbert, in Colorado, which rises 14,440 feet (4,401 m) above sea level.

The lower slopes of the Rockies are covered in forest. Higher up the mountains, meadows are alive with wildflowers and butterflies in spring. Bighorn sheep, deer, and big squirrels called marmots also live there. The highest summits are bare rock that support little life. Rivers tumble down the steep slopes and crash over waterfalls. Lakes lie in the bottom of deep valleys that were carved by glaciers.

Few animals live on the highest mountains, but sure-footed bighorn sheep can climb quickly up the steep, rocky slopes.

Grizzly bears are known for being fierce hunters, but they also eat nuts, grass, and flowers.

26

Beautifully patterned tiger salamanders live in water when they are young. Later they leave the water to live in fallen leaves and soil.

Snow-dusted mountains tower over the still waters of Peyto Lake in Banff National Park. **Sediment** in the water gives the lake its bright blue-green color. The first national park in Canada, Banff has glaciers, hot springs, deep caves, and coniferous forests.

Greenback cutthroat trout live only in clean mountain streams with calm pools.

Baffin Island

Baffin Island in northeastern Canada is the world's fifth-largest island. There is sunshine all day long in midsummer, but the Sun does not rise at all from November until the end of January.

The island is bitterly cold and the temperature stays mostly below freezing. Inland, the treeless **tundra** landscape is too harsh for people to live there, but it's home to herds of reindeer, mouselike lemmings, Arctic hares, and Arctic foxes. Seabirds nest on coastal cliffs, while polar bears and walruses hunt and rest on the frozen ocean below.

Beluga whales are very **social** animals. Dozens or even hundreds swim together as they search for **crustaceans** or fish to eat.

A snowy owl's white feathers blend in with the snow-covered ground.

Fields of cottongrass bloom on the tundra each spring.

Polar bears are excellent swimmers. These huge **carnivores** hunt seals in the water and on the sea ice.

Arctic hares have white fur in winter, which makes it hard for predators to see them. In summer, they have brown fur.

29

Glossary

antlers Branched horns on a deer's head

arable Suitable for growing crops

bacteria Single-celled organisms, some of which cause diseases

birds of prey Birds that kill and eat animals

broad-leaved Having flat, wide leaves

camouflage Colors or patterns that make something hard to see

carnivores Animals that kill and eat other animals

coniferous Having needles and cones instead of leaves; evergreen

coyote A wolf-like wild dog

crustacean An animal, such as a lobster or crab, with an external skeleton but no backbone

delta The area where a river drops mud and sand as it enters a lake or ocean

desert An area that receives little or no rainfall and has few or no plants

eroded Worn away by the action of rain, water, or wind

fossils Animals or plants that died long ago and hardened into rock over time

geyser A hot spring in which boiling water causes jets of water and steam to erupt

glacier A large body of ice moving slowly down a valley

lava Hot, melted rock that erupts from a volcano

manatee An aquatic plant-eating mammal, also called a sea cow

mangrove forests Trees and shrubs that grow in coastal swamps

marsh An area of soft, wet land with many grasses and other plants

molten Turned to a liquid by heat

nectar Sugary liquid found in flowers

nocturnal Active at night

permanently In a way that lasts forever

plateau High, level ground

predators Animals that hunt and eat other animals

prey Animals that are killed and eaten by other animals

rain forest A thick forest that receives high amounts of rainfall

sandstone Rock made of grains of sand or quartz that have been pressed together over time

sea anemone A sea animal that has a ring of stinging tentacles around its mouth

sediment Tiny grains of rock or sand in water

social Liking the company of others

summit The very top

tundra A flat, treeless region of the Arctic

venom A chemical some animals use to poison prey

venomous Producing chemicals that can injure or kill prey

vertical Straight up

Further Information

Books

Kellaher, Karen. *North America*. Scholastic, 2019.

O'Brien, Cynthia. *Pathways Through North America*. Crabtree Publishing, 2019.

Petersen, Christine. *Learning about North America*. Lerner Publishing, 2015.

Rockett, Paul. *Mapping North America*. Crabtree Publishing, 2017.

Websites

www.coolkidfacts.com/mississippi-river/
Read about the history and geography of the great river.

www.kidzone.ws/habitats/rocky-mountains.htm
Find information about the geography, plants, and animals of North America's greatest mountain range here.

www.nationalgeographic.com/animals/index/
Type in the names of animals and get lots of fascinating facts about mammals, reptiles, amphibians, fish, and birds.

www.nps.gov/ever/learn/kidsyouth/learning-about-the-everglades.htm
Get information about the history, people, nature, and geography of Florida's Everglades at this website.

Index